The Secrets in Your Face

Revealing Your Hidden Mysteries

by Patrick Caton

0 43422 69581 2

Cover Design by Design Dynamics.
Typography by MarketForce, Inc., Burr Ridge, IL

Published by Great Quotations Publishing Co.,
Glendale Heights, IL

ISBN # 1-56245-337-8

Library of Congress Catalog Number: 97-77653

Printed in U.S.A.

Dedication

This book is dedicated to
Brian Carey, the hard ways and
people who can roll hard ways.

P.S. This is also dedicated
to everyone at
Teacher's Discovery
except Rick Vess.

Introduction

Subconsciously, we are constantly making judgements about people based on their appearances. Chinese culture began cataloging these physical traits thousands of years ago, collecting and processing them into the science of physiognomy, or face reading. Use this book to analyze the features of people's faces to find out the character of yourself and the people around you. Just remember, everyone is a face reader, to some degree or another, but The Secrets in Your Face will show you how to use this instinctive skill to your advantage!

Note: Don't put too much emphasis on the reading of one feature. Use all the features in tandem to gain an overall understanding of the person's nature.

Table of Contents

The Eyes

The eyes are the most important feature on the face. They "control" the other major features. In fact, they are a constant feature on the face, even as a person ages. Bright, clear eyes are best, because if the eye area is swollen, for example, you will not get an accurate reading.
Do not worry about the color of the eyes, just the shapes and the other features mentioned.

Points to look for

✔ Watery eyes are a sign of a healthy sexual appetite.

✔ Large, wide-open eyes are the sign of a friendly, easy-going nature.

✔ If there is no fold on the eyelid, you are likely to react strongly to an emotional situation.

TRIANGULAR EYES

WHAT TO LOOK FOR

These eyes are alert. The white of the eyes and the iris
have distinct colors.

WHAT IT MEANS

This type of eye signifies success, wealth and prosperity.
You are competitive and goal oriented. You are aware
of what is happening around you before making any
important decisions. You will probably offend others with
your single-minded determination.

WHEEL EYES

WHAT TO LOOK FOR

These have colored lines in the iris. They are known as "angry eyes".

WHAT IT MEANS

Your physical and straight-forward nature can be, at times, over-powering. You are very expressive with your friends and family if you feel it is in their best interest.

FIRE WHEEL EYES

WHAT TO LOOK FOR

Look at the edge of the iris for a colored ring, either light green, red or blue. Sometimes you will notice a light colored ring in the center of the eye.

WHAT IT MEANS

What a hot-head! Your alert nature allows you to find any strengths or weaknesses in others, and you are quick to tell them.

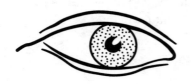 

SAND EYES

WHAT TO LOOK FOR

You will notice flecks of color in the iris. The eyes are sharp and alert.

WHAT IT MEANS

You are never at a loss for words. Your ability to see through an argument makes you good in a debate, but many see you as unsettled and quarrelsome.

MOLE EYES

WHAT TO LOOK FOR
A fleck of color in the white of the eye.

WHAT IT MEANS
You think in the short-term. Be careful: you are tempted to spend money as soon as you get it, but you will have unlucky periods in life. Try to think ahead!

DRUNK EYES

WHAT TO LOOK FOR

Your eyes are bloodshot and you always look sleepy.
The iris slopes down, and the whites of the eyes are yellowish.
The fishtail has several little wrinkles in it.

WHAT IT MEANS

Your sexual appetite is insatiable! Unlucky periods will
follow you through life, but be patient and don't make
any rash decisions.

UNWRINKLED EYES

WHAT TO LOOK FOR

This eye never seems to wrinkle, regardless of the age.
The tail of the eye is rounded.

WHAT IT MEANS

You are intelligent and charismatic. Your ability to persuade
others may cause some troubles in your romantic life.

PEA BLOSSOM EYES

WHAT TO LOOK FOR

The shape of the eye is long and bow-shaped.
The iris and the white of the eye are cloudy.

WHAT IT MEANS

You have an active social and romantic life,
but you need to be more trusting of strangers.
Your creativity is well suited to a career in the arts.

ELEPHANT EYES

WHAT TO LOOK FOR

This eye is narrow and long, with wrinkles above and below the eye.

WHAT IT MEANS

Your sympathetic nature makes you a crowd favorite. Your friends know they can trust you when the chips are down. You bring your creative and enthusiastic nature to any project you are working on.

LION EYES

WHAT TO LOOK FOR

These large eyes are clear in the iris and the whites.
The iris is located at the top of the eye, and there are
several lines on the lid.

WHAT IT MEANS

Your advancement on the job comes from your serious
approach to your career. People like to tap into your
wisdom for judgement on people and situations.

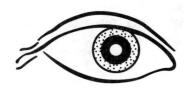 

TIGER EYES

WHAT TO LOOK FOR

The iris has a golden color, and the gaze is steady
and straight. There is a line on the upper lid, but none
underneath the eye. The fishtails are short and scattered.

WHAT IT MEANS

Your good attitude and behavior inspire others to act
sensibly. People tend to take your advice. You can't be
there for everyone, so give yourself time to be alone,
at work and at home.

CRANE EYES

WHAT TO LOOK FOR

These are large eyes. The iris is round, clear and centered in the eye. The shape of the eye is long, with two or more wrinkles on the eyelid.

WHAT IT MEANS

You are honest and straight-forward. Your congeniality is due to your easy-going attitude and your concern for others. You don't just make friends easily, you keep them, too.

EGRET EYES

WHAT TO LOOK FOR

The shape of the eye is long, and the iris or whites look a little yellowish. The iris is located high in the eye, and the eyelid has a long wrinkle. There are no long wrinkles under the eye.

WHAT IT MEANS

You are a loner. You are close to your family, so don't let your independent spirit and anti-authoritarianism keep you from turning to them for help when you need it.

WILD GOOSE EYES

WHAT TO LOOK FOR

The pupils are large, and the iris has a golden tint.
There is a long wrinkle above and below the eye.
The shape of the eye is long and well-defined.

WHAT IT MEANS

Your motto: take it easy! Your contented nature keeps you
from being more ambitious, so you don't take advantage
of promotions and opportunities when they arise. But at least
you have a large number of friends.

SWALLOW EYES

WHAT TO LOOK FOR

These eyes are deep set, have a long line above and below them and are clear and bright.

WHAT IT MEANS

You are trustworthy and faithful. Your word is as good as gold. You will never be wealthy, but you are more concerned with being comfortable.

HORSE EYES

WHAT TO LOOK FOR

The eye is bulging and watery. The lower lid has several folds of skin, and the upper lid is soft. The fishtail wrinkles at the outer corner of the eye grow downward.

WHAT IT MEANS

You have drive and energy, but you never get what you deserve. Don't let personal or professional setbacks interfere with your goals.

LAMB EYES

WHAT TO LOOK FOR

This eye has a dark cast, and the iris is yellowish.
Sometimes wheel-shaped lines are seen in the iris.
The upper lid has a fold, but the lower one doesn't.
The skin beneath the eye is flat and thin, with many lines.
The fishtail wrinkles on the outer corner are scattered.

WHAT IT MEANS

You are a good employee, but never get to enjoy the
fruits of your labor. You always spend your free time
dealing with the unexpected. Trust yourself to get things
done, because you can't count on friends and family to
be there for you.

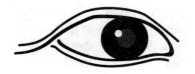 

OXEN EYES

WHAT TO LOOK FOR

The iris and the whites are very clear. The eyes appear large, but do not protrude.

WHAT IT MEANS

You are relaxed, gentle and have an emotionally stable nature. Wrinkles above and below the eye, with fishtail wrinkles which rise at the outer edge, indicate trustworthiness. You are likely to keep your word.

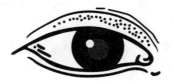 

PIG EYES

WHAT TO LOOK FOR

The iris is dark and cloudy, and the skin on the lid is thick and heavy.

WHAT IT MEANS

You are hot-headed, quick to judge and seldom think things through before doing or saying something. Don't be so rash!

MONKEY EYES

WHAT TO LOOK FOR

The iris is dark and yellowish and located high in the eye.
The shape of the eye is short, and the line above the eye
is rounded and takes a steep slope past the eye corner.

WHAT IT MEANS

Others respect you for your bright, out-going and
courageous attitude. You are the person who likes to
plan and organize everything. You're an optimist.
You also love fruit!

TOP THREE WHITE

WHAT TO LOOK FOR

The iris is on the bottom of the eye, showing white on the top and sides.

WHAT IT MEANS

You are confident and determined, but learn to control your temper. You let others frustrate you if they don't grasp a concept as easily as you or don't do something quickly enough. You are painfully honest.

BOTTOM THREE WHITE

WHAT TO LOOK FOR

The iris is located in the upper part of the eye, showing white on the bottom and the sides of the eye.

WHAT IT MEANS

You know what you want, and you are not afraid to step on a few toes to get it. This self-centered disposition may cause others to resent you.

FOUR WHITE

WHAT TO LOOK FOR

The iris is centered, surrounded by the whites of the eye.

WHAT THIS MEANS

You are quick on your feet, and make the most of the opportunities that present themselves. You lose your temper once your carefully laid plans don't work out as you anticipated.

The Eyebrows

The eyebrows are very expressive. If you are happy, they will be animated when you talk and react to situations around you. If you are sullen, they are low on the brow and close together.

Points to look for

✔ A Well-Defined Eyebrow Bone

✔ A strong and well-defined eyebrow bone is a sign of courage and individuality. Once you've made up your mind, you will not rest until you have convinced others that you're right. You are serious when it comes to your interests: school, hobbies, sports, etc.

UPWARD-GROWING EYEBROW HAIRS

WHAT IT MEANS

These are a sign of courage, but also a bad temper. You are quick to judge and quicker to say whatever is on your mind.

DOWNWARD-GROWING EYEBROW HAIRS

WHAT IT MEANS

You lack self-confidence. You avoid confrontation and the consequences of your actions. Balance in your relationships may be a problem.

CUDDLING HAIR

WHAT IT MEANS

This eyebrow, where the hairs at the top grow down towards the middle and the bottom row of hairs grow up towards the middle, indicate that you worry un-necessarily about routine matters.

SCATTERED HAIR GROWTH

WHAT IT MEANS

This eyebrow, thick and unruly, indicates that you'll have to face unexpected setbacks. These problems may be created by an authority figure.

Thin & Clear Eyebrows

What it means

These light-colored eyebrows show that you are calm and untroubled. You avoid difficult tasks, and when presented with a problem, you pass through it quickly and quietly.

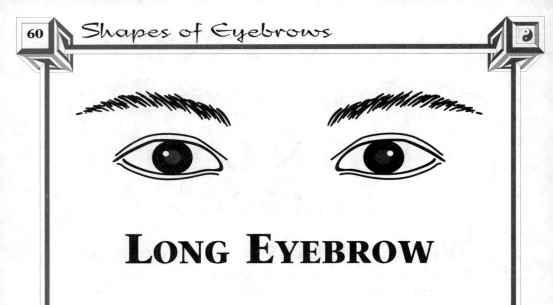

LONG EYEBROW

WHAT TO LOOK FOR

The eyebrow grows beyond the eyetail. The hairs grow in the same direction and are shiny.

WHAT IT MEANS

You have a good intellect and are a talented speaker and debater. You get along well with family and friends. If this is combined with well-balanced facial features, middle age will be a lucky time for you.

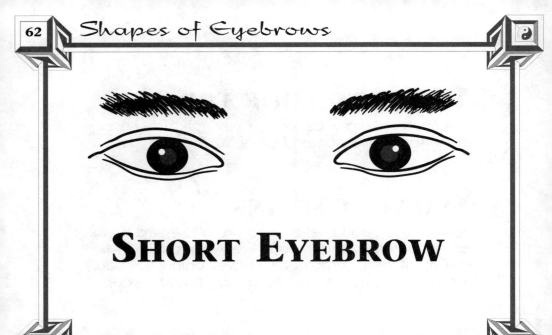

SHORT EYEBROW

WHAT TO LOOK FOR

The hairs are rough and their length is uneven.
The eyebrow is shorter than the eye.

WHAT IT MEANS

You come from a small family, but your efforts
to stay close are strained by arguments and
disagreements. It may take years to find a career
which suits your temperament.

BIG EYEBROW

WHAT TO LOOK FOR

The eyebrow is long, wide and well formed.

WHAT IT MEANS

Your friends appreciate your courageous nature,
since you are the first to stand up for them.
You are not afraid to deal with difficult situations.
You are the dominant partner in your relationships.

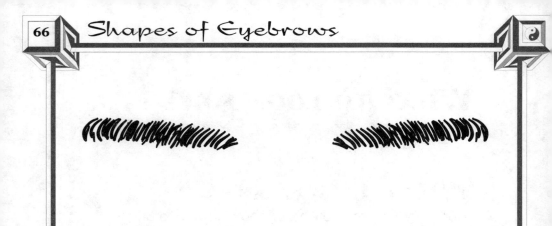

ONE CHARACTER EYEBROW

WHAT TO LOOK FOR

The hairs are thick, and their strong roots can be seen. The eyebrow is straight, medium length and rounded at the end. It is longer than the eyetail, and it looks like the Chinese character for the number 1 (—).

WHAT IT MEANS

You come from a large family with strong, close ties. You enjoy early success in your career and the respect of your co-workers. You will have a long and stable marriage.

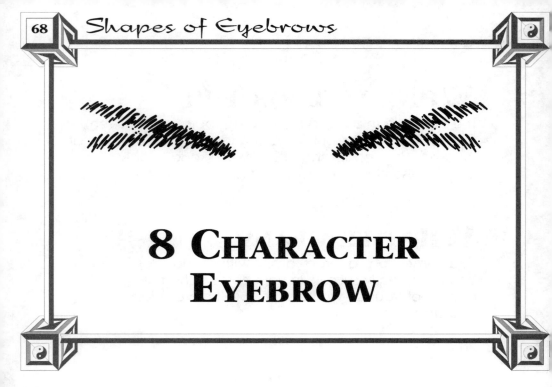

8 CHARACTER EYEBROW

WHAT TO LOOK FOR

The eyebrow is shaped like a "Y", since it is scattered at the eyebrow tail. The hair growth is thin. This eyebrow resembles the Chinese character for the number 8 ().

WHAT IT MEANS

You are a loner. You have a hard time finding a good partner in romantic relationships, but then you find it difficult to relax or socialize with anyone. You will be financially independent, but could be more so if you take advantage of the career opportunities that present themselves. You will live a long life.

GHOST EYEBROW

WHAT TO LOOK FOR

This short, curved eyebrow is positioned low on the browbone. The hairs grow upwards and lie straight, so it looks as if they do not follow the flow of the curve.

WHAT IT MEANS

You are paranoid and suspicious. You don't like others to know what makes you tick, so you appear sharp and antagonistic. You have a difficult time finding suitable careers and romantic partners that match your temperament.

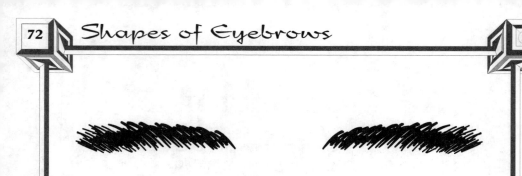

SHARP KNIFE EYEBROW

WHAT TO LOOK FOR

This eyebrow has a sharp head and it widens towards the tail, making it look "dagger-like". The hairs are thick and rough.

WHAT IT MEANS

You are opportunistic, and are always finding ways to turn a profit or gain into an advantage. You are adept at finding an easy way out of any problem or embarrassing situation. Others may see you as arrogant, since you never miss an opportunity to tell others about your good achievements.

ROLLING, CIRCULAR EYEBROWS

WHAT TO LOOK FOR

Dark, thick hairs curl in the same direction.

WHAT IT MEANS

This unusual eyebrow is often seen on the faces of powerful military and political figures. You are destined for great things.

BROOM EYEBROW

WHAT TO LOOK FOR

The hairs at the head of the eyebrow are thick, but scatter as they grow out to the tail.

WHAT IT MEANS

You are from a large family, but distance and financial difficulties keep you from being close to each other. This emotional indifference will carry over to your own family if you aren't careful. You will never be wealthy, but will make enough money to survive.

LITTLE BROOM
EYEBROW

WHAT TO LOOK FOR

This is the same shape as the Broom Eyebrow, but shorter. It does not reach the eyetail.

WHAT IT MEANS

You are impatient and hot-headed, but you're also opportunistic and always find a way to land on your feet. You're no stranger to familial strife, and domestic arguments are commonplace.

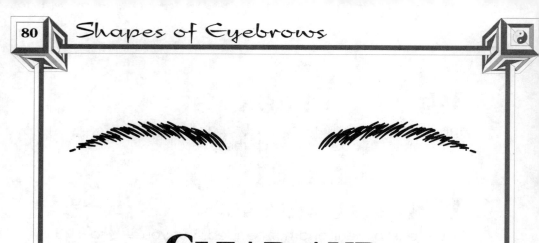

CLEAR AND BEAUTIFUL EYEBROW

WHAT TO LOOK FOR

This eyebrow is long and slightly curved. The hairs arch in the same direction, and the roots are not easily seen. If the eyebrow is short and high but still has the signature hair growth, the reading is the same.

WHAT IT MEANS

You are trustworthy, and everyone knows your word is as good as gold. You are good at compromise and finding peaceful resolutions to others' problems. You will have good fortune in your career and family life.

MORTAL EYEBROW

WHAT TO LOOK FOR

The hairs are long, rough and thick. The eyebrow is short, bushy and wide. The tail grows downward.

WHAT IT MEANS

People see you as a loner, but that's just because you don't like to lower your guard until you know someone. Because of this, you will not have children until late in life. Don't count on parents, brothers or sisters to help you in raising your kids.

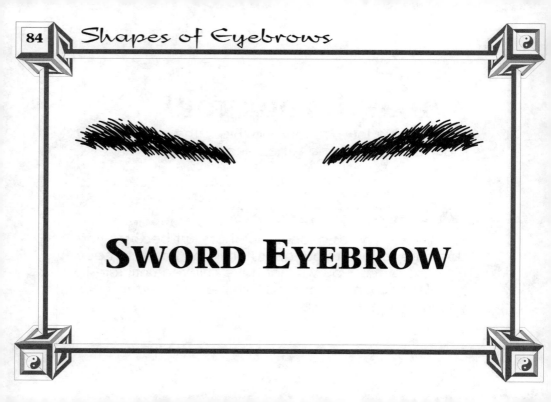

SWORD EYEBROW

WHAT TO LOOK FOR

This eyebrow is long, straight, wide and flat, and it is positioned high on the brow. The hairs grow in the same direction and become thicker at the tail.

WHAT IT MEANS

You are a good judge of character. You are a born leader, and you have the wisdom to run a successful business. You resolve problems peacefully. You will have a long life and a large family.

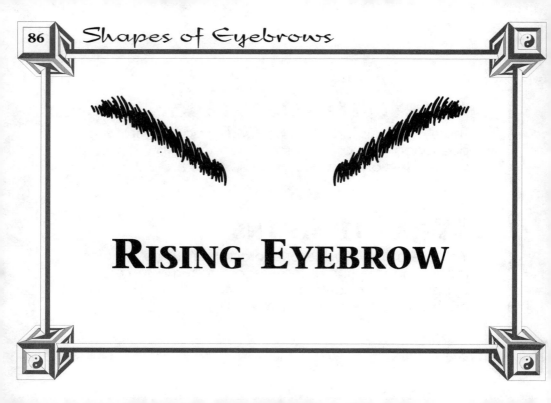

RISING EYEBROW

WHAT TO LOOK FOR

This eyebrow is long, rising evenly beyond
the tail (rising like a long knife).

WHAT IT MEANS

You are determined and have a "never say die" attitude.
People think you are difficult, because you like to have
everything go as you have planned. Your competitive
nature translates into early success, and you will enjoy
moderate success as you grow older. Your family
relationships will suffer as a result of your single-minded
determination to succeed at your career.

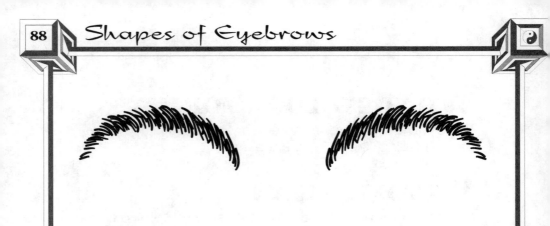

WILLOW LEAF EYEBROW

WHAT TO LOOK FOR

The hairs are easily tangled, and the roots are easily seen. The eyebrow is long and slightly curved.

WHAT IT MEANS

Your popularity comes from your open, friendly and honest character. You are bright and willing to learn. You are socially and romantically active. You have the potential to be wealthy and are helped along the way by an influential friend. You will not start a family until late in life.

NEW MOON
EYEBROW

WHAT TO LOOK FOR

The eyebrow is long, well formed and high above the eye. The hairs are glossy and grow in the same direction.

WHAT IT MEANS

You are thoughtful and honest, and this translates into success at work and in your social circles.
You are from a large, close-knit family.
You will be a devoted partner and a good parent.

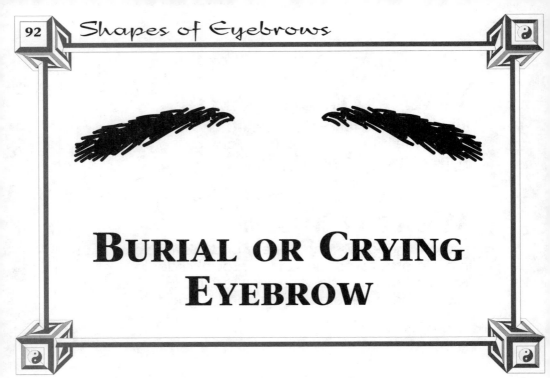

BURIAL OR CRYING EYEBROW

WHAT TO LOOK FOR

The eyebrow head is higher than the tail,
and the hairs grow downward, scattering in different
directions. The eyebrow is shorter than the eyetail.

WHAT IT MEANS

You are difficult person for others to read.
You are quick-witted and use this to make the
most of opportunities which present themselves.
Your success in business may cause others to resent you.

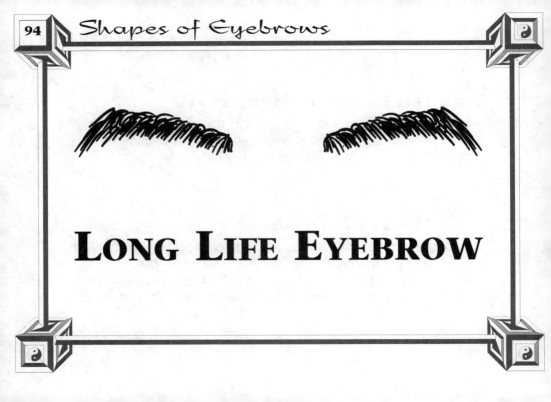

LONG LIFE EYEBROW

WHAT TO LOOK FOR

The body of the eyebrow is wide. These dark and glossy hairs are longer at the tail than at the head. The eyebrow curves slightly downward.

WHAT IT MEANS

Your life will be long and successful. Your creativity is well suited for writing, and you are likely to find fame and fortune in this field. You are friendly and popular with members of the opposite sex.

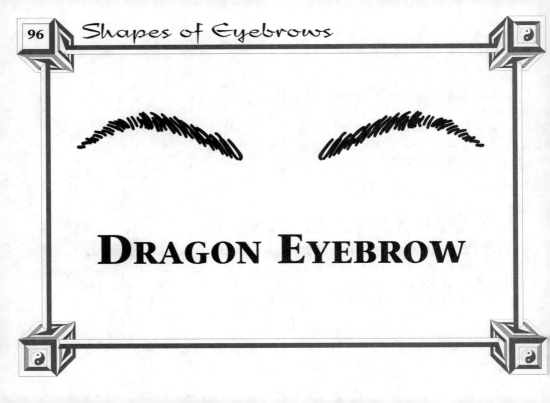

DRAGON EYEBROW

WHAT TO LOOK FOR

The eyebrow rises in a straight line, then slopes downward past the eyetail. The hairs are bright and glossy. This eyebrow has a good overall appearance.

WHAT IT MEANS

You are from a large family. You are clever and have good business-sense. You are ready to speak up if you feel the need, so you take a prominent role in difficult situations. This translates to a life of wealth and the respect of your family and colleagues.

SILKWORM EYEBROW

WHAT TO LOOK FOR

The body of the eyebrow is curled and rises upwards. It's glossy hairs give it a smooth, even shape.

WHAT IT MEANS

You are clever and intelligent. Your friends and colleagues trust you. You excel in a disciplined career field and work well in an office environment. You will seize opportunities during your life which will bring you fame and fortune.

LION-SHAPED EYEBROW

WHAT TO LOOK FOR

The eyebrow curls along its length, and the body is wide and curved. The eyebrow is thick, and the roots are visible. The shape looks like a lion lying down.

WHAT IT MEANS

The angry look this eyebrow can give you belies your thoughtful nature. You follow regimented routines, at work and at home. Others admire your generous nature, but domestic squabbles are common. You will enjoy a long life.

The Lips

The lips define the mouth, which is a good indicator of your character. The size and shape of the mouth show kindness or severity, happiness or depression, selfishness or generosity.

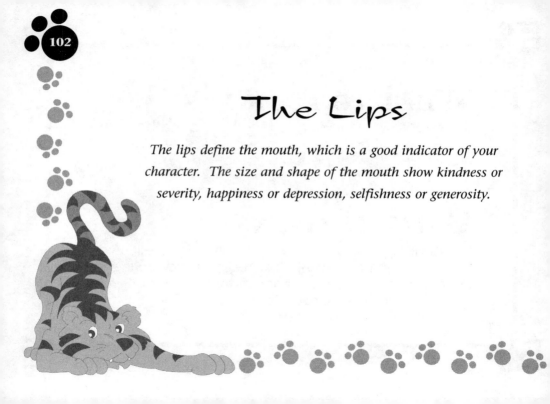

Points to look for

✔ The lips should be red in color and full in relation to the rest of the face. It is luckier to have a large mouth and a small face than the other way around.

✔ Thin lips are a sign of unhappiness or bitterness.

✔ If the bottom part of the upper lip covers the lower lip in the center of the mouth, you are confident, determined and persuasive.

✔ The corners of the mouth are called "sea corners".

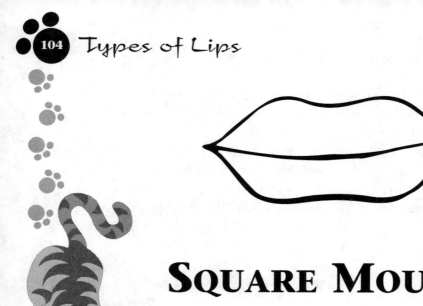

SQUARE MOUTH

WHAT TO LOOK FOR

The lips are thick and red, and the mouth is square.
Your gums remain hidden when you smile or laugh.

WHAT IT MEANS

You are lucky! You earn the respect of others with
your honest nature. Your relationships are firm and stable.

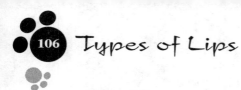

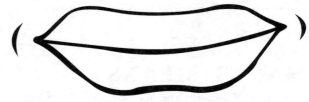

FOUR CHARACTER MOUTH

WHAT TO LOOK FOR

The sea corners are clearly defined and slightly upturned. The lips are thick, moist, red and well-balanced. The shape of the mouth resembles the Chinese character for the number 4 (四).

WHAT IT MEANS

You are clever and creative, and you are probably artistic. You are open and honest with your friends and family. Your generosity and good humor win you the respect of others.

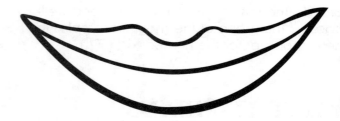

NEW MOON MOUTH

WHAT TO LOOK FOR

The sea corners rise upwards and the mouth is shaped like a new moon. The lips are red.

WHAT IT MEANS

You would be a good fit in a creative career.
Your concentration and tenacity make you a dangerous opponent in a debate.

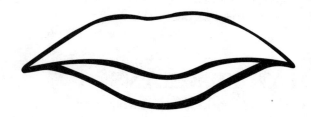

BLOWING FIRE MOUTH

WHAT TO LOOK FOR

Your lips are pursed as if you are about to blow out
a flame. The corners of your mouth slope downwards,
and no sea corners are visible. The lips are thin,
and the upper lip has a sharp point. Your teeth may
protrude slightly.

WHAT IT MEANS

You are a loner. Friendships are hard to come by.
You are resentful because of your distance from others.
Finding friends you can trust are what you need to stop
feeling so rejected.

SCRUNCHED MOUTH

WHAT TO LOOK FOR

The sea corners slope downwards, and your thin and slightly wavy lips give an uneven appearance. They are dry and dull in color.

WHAT IT MEANS

It's not easy for you to trust strangers. You will have a tough time finding a career which suits you. Financial troubles are in your future, but patience will get your through them.

FISH MOUTH

WHAT TO LOOK FOR

The mouth is wide, the lips are thin and the sea corners slope downwards to a point.

WHAT IT MEANS

The only thing harder for you than finding a suitable career is keeping it. Don't depend on financial support from you family—it's not a long term solution.

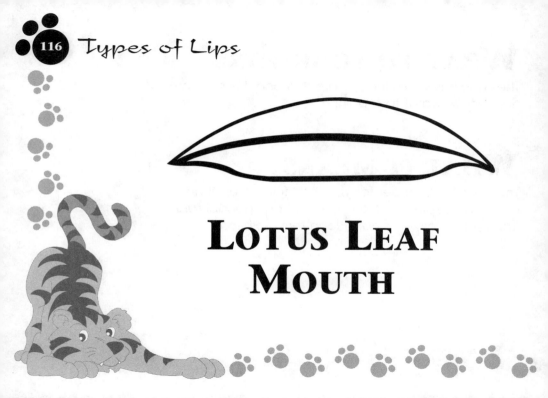

LOTUS LEAF
MOUTH

WHAT TO LOOK FOR

The lips are thin and have a dull color. The mouth is long and the sea corners slope slightly downward.

WHAT IT MEANS

You are uncomfortable talking about your weaknesses, and you may have a tough time admitting them to yourself. Instead of facing criticism, you turn the attention to the affairs of others.

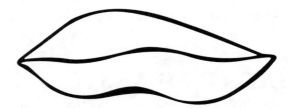

UNBALANCED MOUTH

WHAT TO LOOK FOR

The mouth looks lopsided because one side slopes down and the other slopes up.

WHAT IT MEANS

You love to exaggerate—whether about you or someone else. You're pretty lucky, but you spend any financial windfall as soon as you receive it. You are easily hurt in emotional relationships.

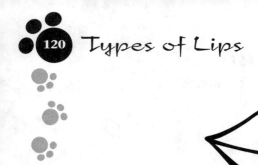

CHERRY MOUTH

WHAT TO LOOK FOR

The size of the face is average, and the corners of the
mouth slope upwards. The lips are red and bright,
and the teeth are small. These teeth are close together
and have a clear, crystal appearance.

WHAT IT MEANS

You are wise and intelligent. Others will come to you
for advice. You are generous and sensitive to the
needs of others. If you are in trouble, an influential
person will help you out.

The Nose

The nose is an important feature of the face, second only to the eyes.
It should not be too thin or too upturned. Look straight at the face to
see if the nose is strong and if the air passageways are clear.
The skin on the nose should be bright and clear, and the tip
should be rounded and muscular.

What to look for:

✔ A plump nose combined with wide nostrils is a sign of a strong sex drive.

✔ A high, thin nose or a nose with nostrils that are visible from the front is a sign of extravagance. You spend money once you get it.

SWORD NOSE

WHAT TO LOOK FOR

The nose is large and high on the face. The bridge of the nose is sharp and hard.

WHAT IT MEANS

Your relationship with your family is unsteady and full of turmoil. You're not unfriendly, it's just that you are uncomfortable in new situations. Don't let yourself become withdrawn at these times.

LONELY
MOUNTAIN
NOSE

WHAT TO LOOK FOR

The end of the nose is very high. The middle of the nose is flat, and the cheekbones are very flat.

WHAT IT MEANS

You try to get the most out of life. You are not as successful as you'd like, but are content with your personal and professional lives. You can't always count on others to bail you out, so learn to be more self-reliant.

HAIRY NOSE

WHAT TO LOOK FOR

The nostrils are large and hairy. The bridge of the nose is strong, but the tip of the nose is thin and flat.

WHAT IT MEANS

You are competitive. You spend money as fast as you make it. Your courageous nature will get you through the tough times. You will be successful in many areas, but have a difficult time maintaining this success.

BUN-BRIDGE NOSE

131

WHAT TO LOOK FOR

The middle of the nose protrudes, so the nose looks large at first glance. But it is actually thin and lacks muscle.

WHAT IT MEANS

You have an honest and humorous character, but your behavior is erratic. Your friends think you are unpredictable. Your energy gets you through the highs and lows you experience at work.

THREE-BENDS NOSE

WHAT TO LOOK FOR

The top of the nose dips in and the middle of the nose protrudes. The end of the nose is sharp and thin.

WHAT IT MEANS

Just when everything is going smoothly for you, something always comes up to knock you off your path. In time you will learn to get through these roadblocks. This keeps your life pretty exciting!

COLLAPSED NOSE

WHAT TO LOOK FOR

The nose is soft, the tip is small and the bridge is flat.
The bridge seems to sink inward and the nostrils are seen
clearly when looking directly at the face.

WHAT IT MEANS

You are opportunistic. When you see a chance to make
some money, you go for it, although it may not always
come out like you planned. It seems as if you never make
as much as you thought you would. You avoid trouble and
don't take on unnecessary responsibilities.

EAGLE BEAK NOSE

WHAT TO LOOK FOR

The nose is thin and the middle protrudes. The tip of the nose is sharp and hooked.

WHAT IT MEANS

You pursue you own interests, enjoy making money and making a name for yourself in the process. Don't forget that others do not share your interests or enthusiasm. You are presented with good opportunities, but they are short-lived.

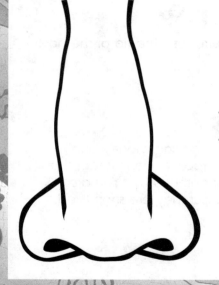

KNOT NOSE

WHAT TO LOOK FOR

The nose has a rounded lump in the middle, and it has the appearance of a knot.

WHAT IT MEANS

You are strong willed and do not like it when others offer advice. You are likely to abandon a project if problems arise, and you don't agree with what others have decided. You are generous, and you perform your work with a lot of energy. The number and quality of friendships you have in life will make up for your lack of wealth.

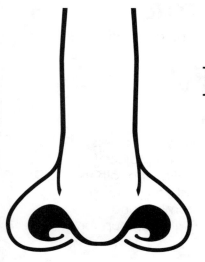

PROTRUDING NOSTRIL NOSE

WHAT TO LOOK FOR

The nose is large, and the tip is rounded and slightly upturned. When looking straight at it, you can almost see the entire nostril.

WHAT IT MEANS

You are laid-back in money matters. If you have money, you spend it, on yourself and others. If you don't have any money, you go without and aren't likely to complain about it.

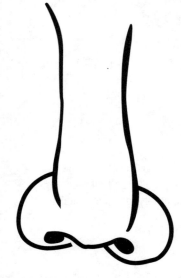

UNBALANCED NOSE

WHAT TO LOOK FOR

One side of the nose is lower than the other. The reading of this nose is improved if the bridge is straight and the tip is rounded.

WHAT IT MEANS

If your bridge is not straight and the tip is not rounded, you will have a difficult time investing wisely or controlling your capital. Expect turmoil in your middle age—rely on your own initiative to survive.

SAGE'S SON NOSE

WHAT TO LOOK FOR

The top of the nose is wide and straight and the line of the nose is well formed and strong. The main body of the nose is long and continues in a straight line to the forehead. The nostrils are balanced and the skin is clear.

WHAT IT MEANS

You enjoy life and everything in it. You have a positive attitude and treat everyone with respect. (What an egalitarian!) Your strong sense of justice compels you to stand up for what is right, regardless of the consequences.

LAMB NOSE

WHAT TO LOOK FOR

The tip of the nose is bulbous, and both nostrils are distinguished. The top of the nose is strong, and the body of the nose is rounded.

WHAT IT MEANS

Your hard work in your career will bring you success. You don't like others getting in your way, and can resent them for it. Your colleagues respect you for your determination and energy.

DEER NOSE

WHAT TO LOOK FOR

The tip of the nose is round, an the body of the nose is slightly indented. The nose still has the appearance of being strong and well formed.

WHAT IT MEANS

You are kind and reliable.   Your word is as good as gold. You are trustworthy (sometimes too trustworthy?) and faithful to family and friends, even those you have known for a short time. You will have a long life and a large family.

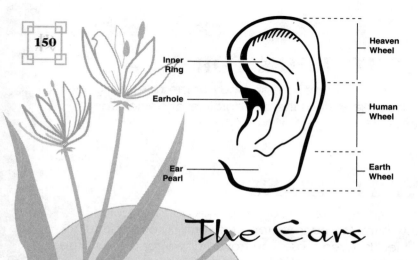

Heaven Wheel

Human Wheel

Earth Wheel

Inner Ring

Earhole

Ear Pearl

The Ears

The ideal ear should grow close to the head and be set on a level between the eyebrow and the tip of the nose. The ear should feel slightly fleshy and the wheel and the inner ring should be an even, smooth shape. This is known as the "Five Fortune Ear". (The five fortunes are: Luck, Long Life, Good Fortune, Peaceful Home and Happy Family.)

What to look for:

✔ If the top of the ear is higher than the eyebrow and the pearl is higher than the tip of the nose, it is a sign of intelligence. You are also an exhibitionist! You'll do anything for attention!!

✔ Caution! If dirty or grey patches suddenly appear on the ear, you are about to enter an unlucky period!

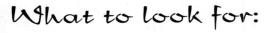

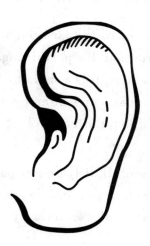

GOLD EAR

WHAT TO LOOK FOR

The ear is set slightly higher than the eyebrow, and the top is close to the inner line. It has a square shape and the pearl feels hard. The outer wheel and the inner ring are distinct. The ear is more pale than the face.

WHAT IT MEANS

You are intelligent and creative, and the world around you interests you. You will enjoy wealth and career success, but only because you are a workaholic. This will keep you from being close to your family.

WOOD EAR

WHAT TO LOOK FOR

The top slopes upwards and the inner wheel protrudes past the outer wheel. The ear is thin and has no pearl. The top is larger than the middle.

WHAT IT MEANS

You put a lot of time into your family and career. Keep it up—your patience will be rewarded with prosperity and happiness in old age.

WATER EAR

WHAT TO LOOK FOR

The ears are thick, set close to the head and are slightly higher than the eyebrow. The pearl is well rounded. The ears are lighter in color than the face.

WHAT IT MEANS

You are quick-witted and intelligent.
This helps you keep your cool when trouble arises.

FIRE EAR

WHAT TO LOOK FOR

The top of the ear curves to a point and is slightly higher than the eyebrow. The inner wheel grows outward past the ear wheel. The ear is long and hard to the touch.

WHAT IT MEANS

You are independent and dislike taking advice from others. Your impatience and determination causes problems in your personal and professional life.

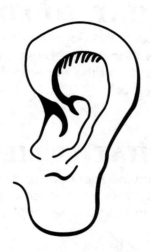

PIG EAR

WHAT TO LOOK FOR

The ear does not have a distinct outer wheel, inner wheel or particular shape. It is soft and thick and may grow either close to or away from the head.

WHAT IT MEANS

You are hot-headed. Regardless how much you try, your anger comes spewing forth. You have a chance to take advantage of opportunities, but you will miss some because you hesitated. You are fortunate with money, but never save or invest it.

PORCUPINE EAR

WHAT TO LOOK FOR

The top of the ear is higher than the eyebrow,
and the upper part is wide and full. The ear is hard
and straight with a strong appearance.

WHAT IT MEANS

You are wise and have good judgement.
You are respected for your vision and capabilities.
You tend to suffer from wanderlust, and you have a
hard time settling down. You are free-wheeling in
monetary matters.

RAT EAR

WHAT TO LOOK FOR

The ear is small, and the outer wheel is tightly curled.
The top of the ear is full and round. The ears are
usually set on the same level as the eyebrow.

WHAT IT MEANS

You are astute and determined. You are always
finding ways to improve your finances, career and
social life. You like to consider all your options before
you act. You never act in haste.

TIGER EAR

WHAT TO LOOK FOR

The ear is thick, hard, small and tightly curled. The outer and inner rings are undistinguished and sometimes uneven and broken. The ear is set close to the head.

WHAT IT MEANS

Your friends and colleagues appreciate your honest nature. You are straightforward and react decisively and impressively. You are a good leader because you know when and how to act, often when others are confused.

Other Titles by Great Quotations

201 Best Things Ever Said
The ABC's of Parenting
African-American Wisdom
As A Cat Thinketh
Astrology for Cats
The Be-Attitudes
The Best of Friends
The Birthday Astrologer
Chicken Soup
Chocoholic Reasonettes
The Cornerstones of Success
Daddy & Me
Fantastic Father,
    Dependable Dad
For Mother, A Bouquet
    of Sentiments
Global Wisdom
Golden Years, Golden Words
Grandma, I Love You
Growing Up in Toyland
Happiness Is Found Along
    the Way
High Anxieties
Hollywords

Hooked on Golf
I Didn't Do It
Ignorance is Bliss
In Celebration of Women
Inspirations
Interior Design for Idiots
I'm Not Over the Hill
The Lemonade Handbook
Let's Talk Decorating
Life's Lessons
Life's Simple Pleasures
A Lifetime of Love
A Light Heart Lives Long
Midwest Wisdom
Mommy & Me
Mrs. Aesop's Fables
Mother, I Love You
Motivating Quotes
    for Motivated People
Mrs. Murphy's Laws
Mrs. Webster's Dictionary
My Daughter,
    My Special Friend
Only a Sister

The Other Species
Parenting 101
The Perfect Man
Reflections
Romantic Rhapsody
The Rose Mystique
The Secret Language of Men
The Secret Language
    of Women
The Secrets in Your Face
The Secrets in Your Name
Social Disgraces
Some Things Never Change
The Sports Page
Sports Widow
Stress or Sanity
A Teacher Is Better Than
    Two Books
TeenAge of Insanity
Thanks from the Heart
Things You'll Learn...
Wedding Wonders
Words From the Coach
Working Woman's World

GREAT QUOTATIONS PUBLISHING COMPANY

Glendale Heights, IL 60139
Phone (630) 582-2800 • Fax (630) 582-2813